Character Education

Courage

by Lucia Raatma

Consultant:
Madonna Murphy, Ph.D.
Associate Professor of Education
University of St. Francis, Joliet, Illinois
Author, *Character Education in America's
Blue Ribbon Schools*

Bridgestone Books
an imprint of Capstone Press
Mankato, Minnesota

Bridgestone Books are published by Capstone Press
151 Good Counsel Drive, P.O. Box 669, Mankato, Minnesota 56002
http://www.capstone-press.com

Library of Congress Cataloging-in-Publication Data
Raatma, Lucia.
    Courage/by Lucia Raatma.
    p. cm. —(Character education)
    Includes bibliographical references (p. 24) and index.
    Summary: Explains the virtue of courage, or the strength to take risks and
complete hard jobs, and describes ways to show courage within the family, at
school, with friends, and in the community.
    ISBN 0-7368-0507-9
    1. Courage—Juvenile literature. [1. Courage.] I. Title. II. Series.
BJ1533.C8 R23 2000
179'.6—dc21   99-048738

Editorial Credits
Sarah Schuette, editor; Steve Christensen, cover designer and illustrator;
    Kimberly Danger, photo researcher

Photo Credits
Archive Photos, 18
Barbara Comnes, 4
International Stock/David Madison, 20
Mary Messenger, 12
Photo Network, 6; Photo Network/Jeff Greenberg, 14
Photri-Microstock, 10
Uniphoto, cover
Visuals Unlimited/Tom Edwards, 8; Jeff Greenberg, 16

1 2 3 4 5 6 05 04 03 02 01 00

Table of Contents

Courage

Courage is the strength to do the right thing even if it is hard. Courageous people try new things even if they are afraid. Courageous people stand up for their beliefs. They are not afraid to be themselves even if others tease them.

tease

to make fun of someone or something

5

Being Courageous with Yourself

Being courageous with yourself means being willing to do difficult things. Courageous people fight their fears. You may be afraid of water. But you show courage if you take swimming lessons. You may not succeed at first. But you are courageous if you try again.

Courage with Your Family

You can be courageous with your family. It takes courage to tell your parents if you did something wrong. You can help family members be courageous. For example, you can help your younger sister get over her fear of trying a new sport.

Courage with Your Friends

You and your friends may enjoy doing the same things. But sometimes you will disagree with your friends. They may want to play in someone's yard without permission. Say no to activities you know are bad. You show courage when you do what is right.

Courage in Performing

Courageous people share their skills with others. Maybe you can sing well or play an instrument. But you may be afraid to perform in front of people. Do not worry about making mistakes. You show courage by performing and doing your best.

Courage at School

You can learn a lot in school. You may be afraid to take a test. Be courageous by studying hard. You may be afraid to give a speech in front of the class. Prepare for your speech. You have nothing to fear if you do your best.

Courage in Your Community

You can be courageous in your community. For example, people in your neighborhood may tease someone. Have the courage to tell them to stop. You may break something on your neighbor's property. Have the courage to admit your mistake.

"Children, if you are tired, keep going. If you are hungry, keep going. If you are scared, keep going. If you want to taste freedom, keep going."
—Harriet Tubman

Harriet Tubman's Courage

Harriet Tubman was a slave. She escaped from her owner. In the 1850s, she worked with the Underground Railroad to help other slaves escape. She made 19 dangerous trips to lead other slaves to freedom. Harriet showed courage by risking her life to free others.

Underground Railroad

a group of people who secretly helped slaves escape to free states before the Civil War (1861–1865)

Courage and You

Courageous people try new things. They face their fears. People who have courage stand up for their beliefs. They are not afraid to be different. They will not do bad things to please their friends. Show your courage by doing the right thing.

Hands On: Interview

Many people are courageous. You and your classmates can interview people to learn more about courage.

What You Need
A pen or pencil
Paper
A person to interview

What You Do
1. Choose someone you know and admire. It could be a grandparent, parent, teacher, or neighbor.
2. Ask the person to tell you about a time when he or she showed courage.
3. Take notes about the person's story.
4. Ask questions about anything you do not understand.
5. Give a report to your class about the person you interviewed.

Words to Know

freedom (FREE-duhm)—the right to say and to do what you want

interview (IN-tur-vyoo)—to ask someone questions to find out more about something

slave (SLAYV)—someone who is owned by another person; a slave works for a master but does not get paid.

tease (teez)—to make fun of someone or something

Underground Railroad (UHN-dur-ground RAYL-rohd)—a group of people who secretly helped slaves escape to free states before the Civil War (1861–1865)

Read More

Hearne, Betsy Gould. *Seven Brave Women.* New York: Greenwillow Books, 1997.
McLoone, Margo. *Harriet Tubman.* Photo-Illustrated Biographies. Mankato, Minn.: Bridgestone Books, 1997.
Moncure, Jane Belk. *The Child's World of Courage.* Plymouth, Minn.: Child's World, 1997.

Internet Sites

The Colors of Courage
http://home.att.net/~RWfreebird
The Life of Harriet Tubman
http://www.nyhistory.com/harriettubman/life.htm
My Hero
http://myhero.com

Index